You Can Make It!
Breaking the Cycle of Abuse

By

C.W. Sistrunk

PROISLE PUBLISHING

Copyright © 2022 by C.W. Sistrunk

ISBN: 978-1-959449-44-7

*All rights reserved. No part of this book may be reproduced or transmitted in any form or by any means, electronic or mechanical, including photocopying, recording, or by any information storage and retrieval system, without permission in writing from the copyright owner.
The views expressed in this work are solely those of the author and do not necessarily reflect the views of the publisher, and the publisher disclaims any responsibility for them.*

To order additional copies of this book, contact:
*Proisle Publishing Services LLC
1177 6th Ave 5th Floor
New York, NY 10036, USA
Phone: (+1 347-922-3779)
info@proislepublishing.com*

PROISLE PUBLISHING

Table of Contents

Chapter 1 1

Fighting's Without, Fears Within 1

Chapter 2 7

The Beginning of Sorrows 7

Chapter 3 23

Why Trim Your Way To Seek Love? 23

Chapter 4 45

The Broken-Hearted 45

Chapter 5 58

God Turns Rough Roads into 58

Beautiful Destinations 58

    Fix Your Dress 60

    Womanhood as a Commodity 63

    Know Your Worth 66

Dedication

This year, 2022, marks 40 years since witnessing the loss of my mother, ***Margaret Thomas Woods***, to the epidemic of domestic violence.

Mom, in celebration of your courageous act in barring violence from our lives. I dedicate this book to you. You paid the price with your own life to keep us safe. You will forever be my example to never be afraid to walk away from violence, no matter what.

Preface

For we wrestle not against flesh and blood, but against principalities, against powers, against the ruler of the darkness of this world, against spiritual wickedness in high places. - Ephesians 6:12, (KJV)

Growing up, I enjoyed watching the theatrics of World Wrestling Federation (WWF) wrestlers like the entertaining Hulk Hogan. I quaked at the intimidating presence of Andre the Giant, mimicked the raspy voice of Randy 'Macho Man' Savage, and dreaded the death toll as The Undertaker took to the ring. I watched anticipating that takedown moment when these wrestlers performed their signature moves to finish their opponents! I loved wrestling so much as a kid that I tried to imitate their moves. It was all staged of course, but it was still exhilarating to watch. Although I was a fan of the spectator sport, it was an entirely different experience as a child with a front-row seat to real-life, violent wrestling bouts in the raised ring of our home. In my youth, I silently watched as my stepfather drew actual blood from my mother and instilled a perplexing mix of fear and love in my heart.

While my stepfather never abused me, I watched my mom endure violent blows from his fist, belt buckles, or whatever he could find at the time to express his anger and frustration. Although hateful to my mother, my stepfather treated me kindly. I felt a kind of bizarre favoritism from him as I suppose my other siblings might have experienced as well. I don't remember a time when he disciplined me with his voice or his belt. He took me places, played with me, and made me feel accepted. This was puzzling to me receiving such tenderness from him after witnessing him exhibit such harmful behavior towards the woman who birthed me. Perhaps I felt that all men walked in such contradiction - loving one minute and harming the next. The reason for this dichotomy within my stepfather would later be revealed.

It was by way of his death certificate that I learned the reason for his dual personality and the cause of my stepfather's death. It was a "self-inflicted gunshot wound to the head due to or as a consequence of schizophrenia paranoid type, deceased at the age of 32." After so many years, I realized that my stepdad wasn't a monster at all. He was a man split in two unable to navigate the rough road he was dealt.

Many years after I witnessed him lift that gun to his head and pull the trigger, I found myself raising my own children and experiencing one abusive relationship after the other. One night, after praying to know why I was going through the abuse I suffered, I dreamt my children and I were being chased by my stepfather who at this time had been dead many years.

To find safety in the dream, I hurried my children down something that appeared to be a pier. It was night and one of my sons slipped and fell into the water that surrounded us. The rest of the children and I worked together to hurriedly recover him to find shelter in a small structure that stood at the end of the pier. My stepfather angrily followed us, walking with a pistol in his hand. Once inside and having nowhere to hide, my children and I fearfully stood face to face with my stepfather who in the dream, positioned himself at the entrance of the structure leaving us with nowhere to run. He didn't say a word and neither did I, but there was no doubt that he was there to inflict harm upon me and my children. He raised the gun in his hand and pointed it in our direction as we cried out for help.

Suddenly, a man who was a member of the local church I attended jumped out of nowhere and shot my stepfather three times center mass. He instantly fell dead. I was relieved that we were no longer in any physical danger, but before I could utter a sigh of relief, I saw a spirit - airy, dark, and looming like smoke but with a human form - rise from the dead body of my stepfather. Before I could say anything, it rushed towards us like the wind. In my astonishment, I was immediately awakened from my sleep. I realized from this dream that it wasn't my physical abuser that I defended myself and my children from it was a spiritual evil at work that sought to kill me and my offspring. I was in the fight of my life.

Unlike WrestleMania in which flesh contends with flesh to overthrow the other, spiritual wrestling is a conflict between the nonphysical in which we contend against demons and resist the ruler of the darkness of this world – Satan. The word wrestle is used in the Bible to denote a contest in which two contenders attempt to overthrow the other. The victor is triumphant when the opponent's neck is locked in his or her grasp. What I've come to know about that dream so long ago is that we have an adversary attempting to overthrow us in our walk with God, in our love for ourselves and our neighbor, in our God-breathed dreams and aspirations, in our relationships and careers. Yet, like physical wrestling, we believers have signature moves – prayer, worship, faith, the Word of God, fasting, thankfulness, and most of all, the name of Jesus.

These weapons of our warfare seem ordinary to the human mind, but they are extraordinary and "mighty in God for the pulling down of spiritual strongholds, casting down arguments and every high thing that exalts itself against the knowledge of God…" (2 Corinthians 10:3-5, KJV). And you know what the beautiful thing about our warfare is, it's already fixed. It's a rigged fight! David says of the Lord in Psalms 18:39-40, "^{39}for thou hast girded me with strength unto the battle: thou hast subdued under me those that rose up against me. ^{40}Thou hast also given me the necks of my enemies; that I might destroy them that hate me." Make no qualms about it. The enemy of our soul hates us. But remember it's a set fight. You want to have the neck of your enemy- of the violent man that has turned your life upside down? I know you're thinking it's your abuser, but it's someone greater operating behind the scenes and he has only come to kill, steal, and destroy. My hope for you as you read this book is for you to turn to God the only one who can strengthen you in this fight. My earnest prayer is for you to believe you have been given the victory over this abuse in your life. Trust God to lead you safely off this rough road, for only he "makes [you] dwell in safety" so that you will "in peace, both lay down and sleep" (Psalms 4:8, KJV). You can make it!

Chapter 1
Fighting's Without, Fears Within

For, when we were come into Macedonia our flesh had no rest, but were troubled on every side; without were fighting's, within were fears… 2 Corinthians 7:5 (KJV)

Receiving a colorful and messy application of nail polish or playing dress up in mom's high heels should have been the business of our seven- and nine-year-old feet. Instead, these little pedes were forced to hurdle barefoot over lifeless bodies in a life-or-death race for which they we sorely unprepared. Forced into darkness, bathed in mud and rain, pierced with jagged rocks, and prodded by pine needles our feet painfully carried my sister and me on an undesired journey away from the one we loved. We were in search of a safe house free of violent fights and crippling fears. Yet, we dreaded the motherless journey we embarked on. It was a rough road that provided the escape from our country home where the unimaginable descended on us like a whirlwind and blew away what little innocence still existed in our early childhood.

A violent twister of abuse swept through our home on a stormy night in December 1982. My oldest sister, Pooh Bear, lay next to me as we fearfully listened to our intoxicated father yell and shout obscenities at our mom through her bedroom window threatening her to let him in. He was incarcerated for a few days after the last abusive episode and somehow, he returned mad and drunk. We were all too familiar with what followed his drunkenness – a night of horror as we helplessly watched him beat mom to her knees. This was not the first time he abused her, but it was certainly the last. Our stepfather wet and raged, kicked down the front door. We stooped hiding behind our bedroom door not sure what else to do. The last time Pooh Bear tried to go for help through the living room window, he slammed it on her fingers. Pooh Bear was always braver than I was; always the one attempting to get help and getting punished for doing so. I learned at an early age to keep quiet and not endanger myself by getting help. I would take these lessons learned and quietly endure the sting of abusive relationships as a young woman.

Dad's profane shouting continued. Then suddenly, we heard it. It was the blast that caused every voice in the house to cease. Even the breath I inhaled retreated inside my throat and refused to respire. We ran out into the hallway where our dad stood frozen in front of us with a gaze that terrified me. He looked down and lowered the gun in his hand toward us in a zombie-like motion. The expression on his face was monstrous and confused. In an instant, he turned the gun on himself and pulled the trigger, repeating the sound that previously sent shockwaves through my heart. I couldn't believe what I was seeing. My dad without a single word raised the gun to his head and pulled the trigger. The walls vibrated, and the room spun out of control. In the next moment, I found myself standing in front of mom who lay on the floor against her bed in a pool of her blood that seemed to thicken after each glance. I approached her, lifted her head, and cried, "Mama! Wake up! Mama! Please, wake up!" Even at that young age, I do not remember being afraid for myself.

What frightened me most was that mom wouldn't wake up. The thought of never seeing her again frightened me. My seven-year-old mind didn't know how to process what was happening. I didn't know what to do. I knew that I didn't want to leave my mom. Leaving her made the journey to safety undesirable. I was not prepared to leave her - dead or alive.

Pooh Bear shook me to get my attention and told me to grab hold of one of our younger siblings. With our younger sister hoisted on my back, I reluctantly followed Pooh Bear as she carried our baby brother on her back. We couldn't carry our little sister, who was only five months at the time. Therefore, we left her behind. I followed Pooh Bear to the front door that now lay on the floor inside our home. The cold rain beat against our faces as we sought to leave and find help from the neighbor next door. She was a sweet old lady who lived alone and until this day, we don't know whether she didn't answer because of fear or if she just didn't hear us knocking. Either way, we were left in the rain. We continued further down that muddy dirt road until we came to Nanny's house where we found shelter from the rain and a phone to call for help.

As I write this, Pooh Bear is before my eyes drenched in rain.

Pooh Bear, I see why you have always been hard and a little rough around the edges. It was because ever since I could remember, you had to be strong. You carried so much on your back, including us, and led us out of the storm, literally. I am reminded of Esau, and how he sold his birthright to Jacob for food. There have been many occasions out of lack and burdensome situations that you could have relinquished you're calling as firstborn. But you answered your calling even though you didn't fully understand it. I'm glad you didn't give up! You led us through the biggest storm of our lives. You were our Moses. I don't have to look back in history to find inspiration. I have it in you. I thank God for your strength, sacrifice, and your love — no matter how tough you've tried to come across, I know your heart and its mush. I love you, Pooh Bear!

Our stepdad's life was sustained for a short time on life support. He passed away at the age of 32 years old. Our mom, Margaret Thomas Woods, was pronounced dead that very night. She was 29 years old.

It wasn't a stranger that caused the greatest grief of our lives. It was the one with whom we lived, loved, and desperately wanted love in return. Although I saw our stepfather beat our mom and knew it was wrong, I still loved him and wanted him to be with us. I thought if we were quiet enough or good enough that his anger would subside. But instead, he became more infuriated, and the beatings continued.

You may be in an abusive relationship right now. You may be thinking, "If I'm quiet enough, good enough, pleasing enough that he will stop the violence." His violent behavior is not about how well-behaved you are or how docile you are. No matter if you tip-toed around the house and never said a word, he will hit you again. Stop beating yourself up trying to fit in to his warped reality. His fists are busy enough to cause your harm. I implore you to leave believing that with trust in God and a plan, you will surely make it!

Chapter 2
The Beginning of Sorrows

All these are the beginning of sorrows. Matthew 24:8 (KJV)

After the death of our parents, it was our grandparents who raised us. Pooh Bear and I didn't learn until years later that the man we called "Dad" was the biological father to our three younger siblings. He was neither my nor pooh Bear's father, but that didn't change the way we saw his parents. They were our grandparents whose memory we hold dear in our hearts.

Our grandfather was not a very affectionate man, but I knew he loved us. He showed it when he poured a saucer full of coffee from his cup as we watched Tom Brokaw on the evening news. He demonstrated it when he altered his life to care for us and give us a home. He possessed a genuine love that still reverberates today. It was seen in his eyes when he'd say, "You're a sight for sore eyes." I didn't understand at the time that he was telling us how he was happy to see us. I had a full awareness that my grandparents loved us. However, even with the deep-seated knowledge and awareness of my grandfather's love, the older I became, the more convinced I was that the love of a father was somehow very different. I imagined a feeling of possession and a sense of security in first knowing that the man I would call father was truly my father, and secondly knowing that he wanted and loved me unconditionally. Nonetheless, I was appreciative of the love, food, shelter, and clothing our grandparents provided for us; but most of all I appreciated the upbringing they provided us in teaching us about our Lord and Savior, Jesus Christ. It is for this they will forever have my respect and my love.

I was baptized when I was eight years old, one year after the death of my mom. My siblings and I attended a Baptist church with our grandmother, and we were taught that the Bible was our foundation for life. Talking to God came naturally. I enjoyed praying, but as a child, I didn't understand the formality of it.

I couldn't remember the *arts* and *thou's* that accompanied so many of the prayers heard at church. Furthermore, I didn't even know what *art* or *thou* meant at the age of eight. I simply wanted to talk to God. My favorite moment of "talking" to God, which most folks consider praying was at night while sitting on our front porch. It was then that the clouds decided to dissipate, allowing God to see me. During the day, it was as if the clouds hid me and the sun gave a glare, preventing God from seeing my true form, or at least in my overactive imagination this was the case. It was at night, sitting on that porch in the country, that I felt close to God and thought in some strange way He was close to me too.

Yet, despite the closeness I felt, there were still unanswered questions. The questions went unanswered primarily because I was afraid to ask. I was taught that questioning God was a sign of disrespect; therefore, I remained full of questions. Why did God allow it? Why did He permit my mother to be taken in such a violent way? As an adult, I've learned that God doesn't look at our asking Him questions as a sign of disrespect. Isaiah 45:11 tells us that God says for us to ask him "of things to come concerning my sons, and concerning the work of my hands command ye me." He wants our questions and I believe He enjoys hearing our voices whether it's to ask questions or give him praise.

After the death of my parents, I was full of fear. I developed a fear of thunderstorms and darkness. The storms reminded me of that murderous night. The darkness brought nightmares and mental images of my stepfather in hell with the devil ripping his flesh from his back. I imagined it was God's punishment because of what he had done. But to see those images as a child often deterred me from wanting to go to sleep or turning off the light. I came to understand that my mother was gone and I was fearful of not seeing her again. We were taught about heaven, and the hope of seeing her again but I had my doubts about that which I will discuss later. For my stepfather, well, my expectations for him were a bit different.

I loved my stepfather, but after witnessing how he took both their lives without hesitation, disrespect and disgust took the place of that love. My hope was for him to be in hell and for years I wished him there believing eternal damnation was exactly what he deserved. The hate I held in my heart for my dad was excruciating and often accompanied by headaches. I soon realized the hate I carried for him – a dead man - was destroying me. He was gone and had absolutely no concern about my feelings toward him. It wasn't as if he was rolling over in his grave tossing and turning about my unforgiveness. There was no avenue for him to make things right and if closure came it was not coming by way of his resurrection. It was my responsibility to simply forgive. But I felt I was letting him off the hook if I forgave him. I felt I was excusing him for taking the life of my mother and leaving us heartbroken. I couldn't forgive him not on my own. So, I escaped inside myself.

In my pre-teen years, I was an introvert. I thought deeply about everything, and every emotion I felt seemed amplified. If I was sad, there was no cheering me. I was where I was until I wasn't anymore. If I was happy, I was extremely cheerful and discovered that this was the place I wanted to live out my existence. But sadness always came causing me to not identify with anyone or anything. God was no longer close to me, or at least I didn't feel that He was. The older I became, the more questions filled my heart, and I no longer wanted to talk to God, I wanted to question Him but felt I could not because of being taught that it was disrespectful. To make matters worse, my grandmother enrolled me and my siblings in a Catholic school. We attended Mass on Fridays and Baptist Church every other day of the week. Talk about confusion! I suppose that's why as an adult, my religious status is non-denominational.

When my mother was alive, it was commonplace for us to be non-celebratory. We didn't celebrate Christmas or birthdays since she raised us as Jehovah's Witnesses. It never occurred to me that we were different until we experienced a different way of life with our grandparents. In my grandparent's custody, we celebrated birthdays and Christmas was a huge event with church plays, presents, and singing. However, the transition of living with my grandparents upon the death of our parents was very hard for me. I missed my mother. I didn't exactly miss our lifestyle because I enjoyed the celebrations and I now make it a point to celebrate every major holiday and birthday. Even still, I miss my mother's presence.

By the age of nineteen, the issues I faced compounded. I was a freshman in college with a 3.6 GPA, and I was very excited about being there. Yet, I was increasingly overcome with feelings of loneliness, sadness, rejection, and hate. My prayers were almost non-existent. The thoughts of my parents, and now my biological father became more and more burdensome. I became obsessed with whether my mother was really saved having learned the difference between a Baptist and Jehovah's Witness.

Somewhere I read that Jehovah's Witnesses rejected the Trinity believing that Jesus was God's Son, but not attributing Him to the divine nature of God. I was taught in the Baptist church that Jesus is the Word, that the Word was with God, and the Word was God. I reconciled that because my mom didn't accept

Jesus for who He really is; she died in sin, and I would never see her again. The thought of never seeing my mother again caused depression and hate to swallow me. In addition to all of this, I learned that my biological father was still alive and lived in a neighboring city. I often wondered why he deserted me or at least that's what it felt like. Why didn't he love me enough to want to know how I was doing? Why didn't he attempt to come for me? I was left with what felt like a giant hole inside. I tried to fill the void by searching out different religions, something that allowed me to hate my stepfather and made me right in doing so. Our grandparents taught that God is love; therefore, I knew that God would not be pleased with me hating my stepfather. I needed something that made all of this make sense.

Sadness, worry, and hate increased in my life to the point of crippling me. Migraine headaches became a part of life. I couldn't carry this weight anymore. At 19 years old while sitting on an apartment balcony during my freshmen year of college, I remembered the God I came to know as a child. I remembered my grandmother who taught us about the Bible and took us to church. I remembered how I enjoyed talking to God as a child and how close I felt to Him. That night, I cried out to God and asked him to help me. I asked him to take away the weight of hate and depression. I no longer wanted to carry it worrying over whether I would see my mom again. I asked God to take it all away. Admitting my wrong for hating my stepfather, I made no excuses for it. The hate was destroying me. My stepfather was dead! He had no concern whatsoever about my heart toward him. The hate I held in my heart only affected me. Sitting on the balcony for what seemed to be hours, I walked away, free of the hate. I failed to let go of worrying about the state of my mother's soul and the fears of my childhood.

Continuing into my second semester in college, I continued to harbor feelings of fear, rejection, and worry. I carried issues into my relationships. Ending my first year at the university, I met a guy whom I'll call Randall. Randall and I became close, and eventually, that closeness led to premarital sex. I lost my virginity three months before my twentieth birthday. I was taught that it was wrong to have sex before marriage and felt that I was going straight to hell for what I had done, but I continued in that sinful relationship, which at the time gave me a sense of affirmation. Randall gave me the affection I so desperately needed. I didn't think about whether he was the man chosen by God to be my husband nor was I mindful of any consequences that would come about because of this relationship. The only thing on my mind was that I no longer felt the pain of rejection or endured the whirlwind of loneliness. We were more than friends, and I felt loved. However, I would not learn until many years later that it didn't love but lust that I felt, which created a false sense of acceptance. The tricky and sad thing about lust is that if you're not careful, it can be misinterpreted. Remember that love is patient, but lust is always in a hurry for fear its momentum will be lost. It's not concerned with what is right and holy in God's eyes. Its only concern is immediate gratification.

From my first sexual experience, I became pregnant, and my fears compounded. How would this child be cared for? These fears were garnished with a sense of shame. My grandparents were alive at the time, and sex before marriage was deemed unacceptable. In my eyes and no doubt in theirs, my purity was gone forever. Since I was a little girl, I wanted to be married with children, and because I was with a child and not married, I possessed a great shame in addition to my many other issues. I contemplated abortion and even found myself within the walls of an abortion clinic.

Randall and I were both afraid not only at the thought of how we would care for and provide for this child, but also of informing our Christian parents and grandparents that I was pregnant. It was decided that I should have an abortion. When we approached the abortion clinic, we saw people outside protesting. One of the protestors handed me a brochure. Nervously, I reached out my hand to take the brochure, and tucked it safely away in my pocket. I didn't know what to expect. I convinced myself, or so I thought, that this was the right thing to do; but my heart was sure I was wrong. Randall and I entered the clinic together.

A heaviness descended on my shoulders like a ton of bricks. Was I making the right decision? Surely, I was making a decision that would totally secure me in the jaws of hell forever. The palms of my hands felt like water was running over them. As I sat down on the sofa in the lobby of the abortion clinic, I reached for the brochure the protestor handed me as I approached the abortion clinic. The images on this brochure were amazing and terrifying. Tears filled my eyes as I gazed at pictures of babies - fully developed dead babies "Never! I will never kill my baby," I said to Randall as I ran out of that clinic. I asked God to forgive me for even going to that place. Whatever I had to do I would do, but I would not go through an abortion to rid myself of the responsibility that I made my own. Randall and both withdrew from school and moved in together. While I packed to move, I again became very aware that I was dead wrong. I convinced myself that we would get married and that we wouldn't live in sin long. The funny thing is, I realized that if I wasn't pregnant, I would not have considered cohabitating with or marrying Randall. Nevertheless, we both agreed that marriage was the next logical step. It would be a stride we would never take.

My first child was born in 1995. Randall and I, now engaged, moved to Florida with our new baby to plan our wedding; however, during our planning, everything fell apart. He was cheating and I became pregnant for a second time. This time I did the unthinkable. I had an abortion. You might be asking, how could I have gone from an emphatic no to actually go through with an abortion? Desperation causes you to do some crazy things whether negative or positive. At this point in my life, having another child was unimaginable. So, why engage in sexual activity that can produce the very thing you find unimaginable? I wish there was a simple answer to that question. All l know is that this relationship feeds a void in me if only for a little while. But the price of this void filler came at a hefty cost. It cost me the life of my child and my own self-respect in that I stayed with a man who cheated several times.

After the abortion, I cried for days and bore the guilt of what I had done. I was becoming more and more emotionally dependent on Randall. I gave him a burden that should have never been his. My heart looked to him to alleviate the loneliness and rejection I felt from the absence of my biological father. My heart looked to him to calm my fears. I gave him the responsibility of being God in my life, but I didn't realize it for years to come.

After some time, Randall and I broke off the engagement, but I continued to live in Florida. I re-dedicated my life and began going to church regularly. It was in the church that I received the Holy Spirit. I read about it in the Bible, but never personally experienced it until that Sunday. After the sermon, the preacher wanted to take time to be silent because he sensed there was something that the Holy Spirit wanted to do. We were told to meditate on Jesus. My prayer at that moment was that God would touch me. As I sat there in that church pew, it was as if I was sitting beside myself, observing myself. I cried out with such a loud wailing voice. It was unlike anything I'd ever experienced. The presence of God became real to me at that very moment. Once the outcry was over, peace filled my body like a warm blanket covering my soul. I knew it was

God. I felt as if I was intimately acquainted with the God of my grandmother. It was an indescribable moment.

After this experience, I continued going to church, and things were going well. I read my bible more and more. I came across Acts 2:21 which reads, "And it shall come to pass that whosoever will call upon the name of the Lord shall be saved." That was it! That was the reassurance I needed to settle within myself that I would see my mother again. At that moment of reading that scripture, it didn't matter whether she had a full understanding of Jesus' divinity. All that mattered was that she called on the name of the Lord.

Things were looking up! I prayed that God would open a door for me to return home because I missed my family. Sure enough, He did. He opened the door for me to transfer my job back home to Alabama. Once home, I continued to read the Word, but I had not found a church home yet, and I knew that it was crucial for me to do so. Visiting different churches in the area, nothing drew me. It was at this time that the feelings of loneliness and rejection resurfaced. The same issues were still there because I never dealt with the problem and allowed God to heal me. The rejection that stemmed from my biological father was still very much alive in me. I believed that I received the Holy Spirit, and I also believed that my deliverance was already accomplished in Christ. But why were these feelings still there? Why was I still dealing with past demons?

Chapter 3
Why Trim Your Way To Seek Love?

Why trimmest thou thy way to seek love?
Jeremiah 2:33A (KJV)

For several months I was without a church home. Clubbing replaced church. My sisters and I ended up in a nightclub from Friday through Sunday. Clubbing was initially uncomfortable; I'd never gone to a club before. But the more I went the more comfortable I became. The nightclub visits were frequent, and the church visits were nonexistent. I was out of God's will at this point, and spiritual blindness once again set in.

10:00 p.m. was our usual time to hit the nightclub. It was at this time that the partying was high, and the people were full of alcohol. Needless to say, I became a very relaxed Christian. Taking time to read the Bible was few and far between. I embarked on life as if nothing was wrong. It was the attention that I sought, and it was in all the wrong places where I did my seeking. I would spend my weekend partying and my weekdays depressed. I heard talk about my biological father and was told that I had several half-brothers and a half-sister. I met one of my half-brothers that lived in my mother's hometown. I immediately saw myself in him, and we talked as if we'd known each other all our lives.

One day, he suggested to me to meet our dad. I was quite nervous at the idea thinking, *What if he dislikes me and doesn't want to see me?* Nevertheless, because of curiosity, I decided to meet him. Before seeing our biological father, my brother and I agreed not to tell him who I was. We wanted to observe what he had to say after seeing my face. My father stood before me – a short, stout, dark-skinned man - expressing how much I reminded him of someone. I surveyed him to see if I saw anything about him that seemed familiar to me. Did I have any of his expressions; did I stand like him? Did I have his smile? The only thing I saw we had in common was his skin tone. He continued to say how I reminded him of someone from his past. I thought, *really*? Finally, after keeping him in suspense a while, my brother told him who I was, and I confirmed it. He smiled and put his arms around me. I was happy that he seemed pleased to see me.

Our visits continued after that. We had conversations about different things, but the real issues never came up. We never discussed why he never came around or why he left. The feelings of rejection, disappointment, and depression subsided. However, I soon realized that the visits were one-sided. He made no attempts to see or call me. If we saw each other, it was because I wanted to and made the effort to do so. Eventually, hurt, rejection, and disappointment resurfaced in my heart because of the lack of pursuit on his part. The visits ended, and since that time, he did not attempt to see or contact me. Years later, he suffered a stroke and was left disabled. The emptiness, disappointment, and hurt that I felt from never receiving the active love of my father would cripple me for years to come. Yet, I tucked the feelings of rejection away once again and carried on with life as if nothing was wrong. The road I once traveled toward salvation had become trimmed by my thirst for love in all the wrong places.

I met another young man who I'll call "Trey." Trey and I began dating, and the sin of fornication began with him. The sex created in me a feeling of acceptance and love, but in reality, it was all a lie. I now know that my desire for sex was a symptom of a much deeper issue of rejection. It was lust, a counterfeit of love that I allowed to blind me! I prayed a little here and there; but for the most part, the Word became obsolete, and I continued in this sinful relationship.

The courtship started off well enough, or at least my blinded mind was convinced that it did. Then one night we argued about a trip to Florida that I planned to take with my baby to visit her grandparents. We were driving back from visiting Trey's mom when he began telling me how he wasn't going to let me go to Florida. We went back and forth arguing about what he wasn't going to let me do. We were on our way to my cousin's home when he quickly made a U-turn. I asked him where he was taking me, and he told me that I would see him in a minute. It was dark and cold. I just wanted to get home. He made a turn. The tires exchanged the smoothness of the paved road for the coarseness of gravel. I didn't know what to expect, but I didn't have a good feeling.

The car barely stopped rolling when I opened the door. I noticed we were at the edge of the water, parked down a boat ramp. I immediately started running and couldn't see anything. I didn't get far before Trey grabbed me and pulled me back to the car thrusting me against the passenger car door. He then shoved me inside the car through the driver's side injuring my leg on the gear shaft while yelling at me. Once inside, he commenced hitting me telling me how he was going to kill me. It was at this point that I cried for him not to hurt me. Trey explained to me in great detail what he was going to do. He said that he would use one of the stones next to the car to pound my head until I lost consciousness or died. He went on to say how he would lay my body in the backseat and push the car into the river.

I prayed silently and frantically, "Lord, please don't let him do this." While I was silently praying, Trey smoked a cigarette. It was his habit to smoke and drink daily. After taking his final draw, he threw the butt out and said with a shout, "Wait! That's evidence!" He didn't want to leave anything linking him to what he was about to do. Needless to say, I prayed even more. I began talking to him as nicely as I could. I begged him not to do what he planned. He said he had to at this point because he knew that things would never be the same with us. He said that I would want to leave him. I convinced him that I loved him and that I would not leave. I told him that I wouldn't tell anyone anything. I said whatever I needed to say to convince him to forsake his sick plan. After some time, he finally put the car in reverse and backed out.

He drove to my cousin's home and told me that if I went inside and said anything to anyone, he would kill everyone inside the house, including my baby girl. I had no doubt in my mind that he would do what he boasted. Of course, for the safety of my family, I kept quiet.

All the lights in the house were off, and the living room was empty. My cousin was already in bed, and my baby girl was with her. Trey decided to stay overnight perhaps to ensure that I said nothing. I headed to the bedroom, with him close behind. He grabbed me and began kissing and touching me. The smell of cigarette smoke and alcohol oozed from his skin and mouth. The closer he came to me, the more repulsed by him I became. I pushed him away and walked out to the bedroom. The look on his face signified his anger. He hit me in the face knocking me to the bed. He held a razor blade to my neck and told me that if I didn't have sex with him, he was going to cut my throat. I looked at him and replied that he would have to do just that to have sex with me. I did all that he asked up until that point, but I could not bring myself to freely have sex with him. He began to choke me and by the grace of God, he stopped; he just stopped. He rolled over and almost immediately fell asleep. I figured the alcohol was taking its toll.

Fear interrupted the fatigue I was feeling. Terror had taken over my heart and my mind. There was no way that I could relax enough to close my eyes. When I was sure he was fast asleep, I grabbed my baby girl's book bag from the closet, packed it with a fresh change of clothes, and waited for daybreak. I was afraid to leave that night because I thought that there would be a great commotion after waking my baby girl. There was no doubt that she would cry, causing my cousin to wake up and drown me with all kinds of questions. There was no doubt in my mind that Trey would wake up and kill us all.

The next morning, the plan was to leave like I was off to work and then make my escape to Florida; but he had a different idea. To ensure that I would not attempt to go anywhere, he commanded that he take me to work. God knows I wanted to break down in tears at that moment. I had to think fast. I knew I didn't want to say no because I felt that if I said anything opposite to what he wanted, he would get upset and hurt us, so I held my peace. I said okay, and we left. I had a plan in mind; so, I asked him to go by the daycare first to drop off my baby girl. I wanted to make sure she was safe and that he had no access to her. Once inside, I asked the director to release her to no one but me. If anyone else tried to pick her up, she was instructed to call the police. I went back out to the car, and he took me to work.

Once we arrived at my office building, I opened the door, and he quickly came around to the passenger side. He apologized to me for what happened the night before and told me that he would return to take me out to lunch. In my mind, I knew there would be no lunch. Once inside the office building, I headed directly to my supervisor to tell her what happened. By that time, the young man drove off. My boss instructed me to call the police for intervention. I was told that because they didn't attack me in their jurisdiction, the only thing that could be done was to arrest Trey for a stolen vehicle. So, I reported my car stolen. I told the police that Trey was coming around noon to take me to lunch. The officer told me not to worry, that I would have my car back and be safe.

When Trey arrived at noon in the parking lot of my workplace, the cops encircled him. I was given my keys, and Trey was driven off in the back of one of the patrol cars. I never filed any formal charges against Trey which, looking back, was a mistake. At that time, I reconciled in my mind that I would stay away from him, and so I did. Trey continued to abuse women and some years later, he was arrested, charged, and convicted for murdering the mother of a young woman he was dating.

I realized a few months after leaving Trey that I was pregnant. I again contemplated abortion, but could not go through with it. I could not bear the idea of going through the emotional distress I'd previously experienced. After seven months of pregnancy, I was told that I was having twins. I was fearful and excited at the news of having twins. I gave birth to my twins on Thanksgiving Day 1998. They were the most handsome boys I'd ever seen. I was indeed grateful for God's gifts to me. My prayer was for their lives to be blessed even though I was far from being whole or righteous.

Remembering how the inside of a church looked became difficult for me. I had no communion with God and after the birth of the twin sons, I was in a constant state of depression. During this time, another man came along who I'll call, "Jake." I was a bridesmaid at my cousin's wedding, and Jake was assigned to escort me. He found the accompaniment as an occasion to flirt, but I ignored him. By this time, I worked at a local plant that made helicopter parts. I worked very late hours and was exhausted from working and taking care of my now three children. One night, a coworker insisted he had someone perfect for me and asked if I would mind meeting him. I obliged, and he scurried off to bring this man to me. I looked up, and to my surprise, it was the same hazel-eyed man that escorted me to my cousin's wedding. I allowed myself to take a second look at him, and we began dating.

I was still making weekend visits to the club, but after spending time with this man and seeing how he showed me great attention and concern, I became convinced that he wanted more from me than just dating. He would often read the Bible, and even though I was far from the Word at this point, I was glad to finally see a man who seemed to acknowledge God in his life. So, I left the club scene, became domesticated, and began reading the Bible myself. Neither of us attended church. My heart was so hardened by my sinful acts that God was not a high priority in my life anymore. I figured I could get by with an occasional reading of the Word but deep down I knew God was not pleased. After nearly a year of dating Jake, I became pregnant with another child, and once again I was scared. I hear the question forming in your mind. Why didn't I use protection or birth control? I was afraid of birth control because of all the horror stories. I didn't want to die of blood clots, and I didn't want to become obese. To be honest, I compromised myself in so many ways that when bringing up the case for the use of a condom to my partner, I was always defeated by whatever excuse I was given not to use one. I wasn't mindful of the consequences of my actions until after the fact. I just wanted to feel loved. It's twisted and distorted, I know, but that was my frame of mind for years.

My boys weren't even a year yet, and there I was pregnant again. I panicked! I convinced myself that I could not have this child and decided to have an abortion. I didn't recall the years before when I had my first abortion. I didn't remember the pain and anguish I felt from killing my baby. Sin will blind you so much and cause your heart to be so hardened and fearful that you forget about the consequences. Nevertheless, I had an abortion. The consequences of having this abortion were soon realized.

Nights became a terror for me once again. Images of babies drenched in a blood filled my dreams. I was afraid to go to sleep. Depression was an everyday occurrence, and my life was far worse than I ever imagined. Jake became abusive and relied more and more on alcohol. Whether I was asleep or facing life with my eyes wide open, life was difficult. I was in a perpetual hell and this hell became more evident when Jake's fist first collided with my face.

The very first time Jake hit me, I was driving, with my children in the backseat. He exclaimed that I knew he was hungry and that I should have stopped to get something to eat. I stopped the car at a red light, stepped out into the street, and with the courage of a giant retorted,

"Come on! If you want to fight, I'm ready!" He laughed at me and told me to get back in the car. I looked back at my children, and they had tears in their eyes.

At that moment, I felt utterly defeated. I made a stark fool of myself for making such a terrible gesture, getting back into the car, and allowing all this to unfold in front of my children. The abuse became more frequent and more intense. However, the first year of our relationship was abuse-free. Looking back, that first year was the year he drew me in. There were signs here and there, but I mistook the signs as love and attention. One night, while out with some of my family at the club, Jake came to my sister's home. Certain family members and I arrived around three o'clock am. He was sitting in his car. I approached him and asked him if anything was wrong. He told me he was just waiting on me. I thought that it was too cute that he waited for me so late. I said to myself, *this man loves me!* It never occurred to me until years later that it wasn't cute, and what he was doing was called stalking. But I failed to see the signs. I remember thinking how the abuse was so unlike Jake and making excuses for him by saying that he just had a bad day and things would get better.

The first year we dated was unlike him. He was mimicking what I wanted and not portraying the person that he truly was. The last four years of our relationship revealed his true form. Later, I learned from others in the community that he had a history of abusing other women. Yet I didn't leave. Afraid of being alone and convinced of Jake's lies that no one else wanted me. I had a distorted self-image. When I looked at myself, all I saw was a mess. I became pregnant for the fifth time and had no intent to relive the terror of abortion.

Seven months into my fifth pregnancy, I had a car accident. I started the day preparing to take my firstborn to the bus stop. We were running very late and had to rush to try to make it in time. Because of the rush, I didn't take the time to make sure my oldest daughter was securely fastened, and I didn't think to secure myself. We were about ten miles into the trip when we entered a curve, and I saw a sheet of loose gravel spread all over the road. As I hit the brakes, the car began to slide out of control. We hit an incline on the side of the road, and that sent the car tumbling through the air. "Lord have mercy," is the last thing I remember saying. I'm not sure how many times the car flipped.

When I resumed consciousness, I realized that I was lying in a bush of briars. My oldest daughter miraculously came away with only dirty shoes. The baby I carried was fine, but I suffered a broken pelvis and collarbone, with multiple bruises and scratches. Nevertheless, I had my life, and that was a miracle for me. It was a great demonstration of God's mercy. In a loud voice, God was saying, "Come back to me," and I got the message loud and clear. Hospitalized for a month and a half, I jumped into the Word daily

I gave birth to my baby girl in the year 2000. Jake and I continued in that train wreck of a relationship, but I knew that God started a change in me. After my recovery, I began going to Greater New Life Church International in Tuskegee, Alabama. It was at this church that my life began to change. The more I continued in the Word, the Lord softened my hardened heart. The more I sought God, the more light began to filter into my mind. I began seeing myself as Christ saw me - fearfully and wonderfully made. God had a future for me that I needed to realize for myself. I was excited about the Lord, but there was still something that held me in the relationship with Jake. I needed deliverance.

Jake gave me an ultimatum. I was told to either choose him or the church. When I told him that I wasn't leaving the church, he grabbed me in front of my children and choked me. Jake's heart was not for God! It didn't matter how much he read the Bible. He was not allowing Jesus to penetrate his heart, and neither was I until I almost lost my life in the car accident. Jake's Bible reading was only a religious ritual. He had no spiritual fruit in his life. He was just as needy emotionally as I was. Yet, God had begun a change in me after that car accident by turning my affection toward Him. I was hoping that it didn't come to almost losing his life for Jake to realize his need for God as well. We both harbored so much hurt. It was going to take the hand of God to deliver us.

When I told Jake that I would never leave the church, the abuse worsened. The more I developed a relationship with Christ, the more freedom I received, but I still desired to have a good relationship with Jake. I know it sounds crazy but I still didn't want to be alone. I prayed more and more and asked God to allow me to penetrate Jake's heart. I thought that if I stayed, I could witness to him and bring him into the family of God. This was another lie of the enemy. As a saved woman, once you've compromised yourself and remain in a sexual relationship with someone who is not your husband, your witness becomes ineffective. You will lose more than you bargain for and will gain nothing but heartache. You can't save a man from hell by jumping in the pit with him. Trust God to cleanse you, and keep you from habitual sin. Use the rope of prayer to pull him out; but please do not attempt to pray for a man out, hoping that he will wed you. First, be concerned about an individual's soul, and let God handle the rest. As a single woman, focus your energy on the kingdom of God, and He will give you rest. Offer salvation to everyone, without any expectations from anyone except God.

After my prayer that God would allow me to penetrate Jake's heart, I heard the voice of God so clearly. He said, "I am God, the Creator of the universe and all that exists. If Jake has not allowed me to penetrate his heart, who are you to do what he has not allowed me to do?" God later confirmed this to me through a scene in one of my favorite films, *The Godfather Part III*. In this scene, Michael is speaking to the priest. They are standing at a fountain, and the priest picks up a rock. Basically, the priest tells Michael to observe the rock. The Priest tells how this rock has been sitting in the water for years. Then he cracks the rock open and says, "But look on the inside, it is completely dry." He goes on to say that many men sit under the word of God and in His presence, and it never penetrates. From that point on, I stopped asking God to help me penetrate Jake's heart and asked for a closer relationship with Him for myself. I also prayed that God would save Jake, but this time with the hope that God would deliver me from Jake and help me realize the strength that Jesus had given me.

I remember the final abusive episode. I was lying in the bed nearly asleep, and Jake wanted to argue about something so minute that I do not recall the subject of his quarrel. Looking back, I guess the thing that enraged him more was the fact that I ignored him. All of a sudden, he leaped on top of me, held down my arms with his knees, and commenced to pound my face with his fist. I found reprieve only in his pauses to yell and cuss at me. I looked into his eyes and saw something familiar. His eyes reminded me of the eyes of my stepfather; the wild look he had after he shot my mother. I was frightened! He told me how no one else would want me with four kids. He told me I was nothing without him and continued to beat my face. It seemed like an eternity. He stopped only because of tiredness, and I ran to the bathroom afraid but with clarity.

It was then that I finally realized that my life was meant for something more. At that moment, I believed that I was not a punching bag. I was made to receive love, not the bounding of someone's fist. I believed that I was made to be cherished and appreciated, not diminished. I believed in the promise God made that I would lay down in peace without fear of violence.

Standing behind the locked bathroom door and facing myself in the mirror, I beheld a face I did not recognize. My nose was bloody, my left eye was swollen with bloody cuts. I couldn't look at myself. I sat next to the commode, gripping its base. That night will always be remembered as my awakening. The last night I endured abuse of any kind. The night I finally realized that I wasn't loved or cared for. My mind was awakened to greater self-awareness and to the guilt of allowing my children to be exposed to the unfortunate cycle of abuse. The poem below is appropriately called, "The Awakening."

As his fist strikes my face, a fear that is incomprehensible swallows my mind but not before enlightenment has time to pour in its light. All at once I finally realize this is not love! My face balloons to a shape unrecognizable. The same hand that repeatedly hit me moments ago now seeks to console me and dry my tears. How is this possible? This is not love. I pull myself away and take refuge behind a locked door. Tightly I clutch the cold porcelain reservoir. I do not seek to anger him by my leaving. I not only have myself to consider but also four little ones whose feet are not as fleeting. So, I am still myself. As I lay at the edge of the bed with my body constricted as a boa, he asks, "Do you want me to put off work today?" "No," I replied and in the back of my mind, I have a plan. As I watched the daybreak and my freedom fast approaching, my mind is at peace. His engine roared and the tires spun, this was my signal that it was safe to move on November 1, 2004, which was the day I literally said goodbye to my yesterday.

Chapter 4
The Broken-Hearted

The Lord is nigh unto them that are of a broken
heart; and saveth such as be of a contrite spirit.
Psalm 34:18 (kjv)

I was afraid to go back to Jake. I feared reliving the life of my mother and experiencing the death that she suffered as a result of domestic violence. However, I also dreaded being alone and facing my own demons of rejection and loneliness. During this time, I was employed with a local law firm and attended school full-time to obtain a degree in paralegal studies. My boss at the law firm knew of the abuse that was going on because of the obvious physical signs and he warned me to leave my abuser. In order to quiet his questioning of me, I told him that I left the relationship and would not return. When I called out of work and showed up the next day with a black eye, he was furious! His assistant came over to my desk and told me that he was going to fire me; she expressed her sorrow for what happened to me and wanted to give me a heads-up. I was devastated and didn't know what to do. In the middle of my devastation, I remembered King Hezekiah in the Bible and how he humbled himself, and God added fifteen years to his life. I was no King but I figured if it worked for him why it shouldn't work for me? I needed more time on this job after leaving a man who provided financial assistance. Desperate for direction, I entered my church with a black eye and found the courage I needed to fast for three days without food. It would be 4 days later that my boss approached me. On the third day of the fast, God told me what to do. He told me to write a letter. When I was done typing the letter, I proofed it for any errors. I was floored. As I read it, I said to myself, *I did not write this.* The letter was perfect.

The next day I was called into the office of my boss, and he chewed me out. He called me out on the lie I told making his disappointment and disgust for me as clear as day. But I sat there and took it without saying one word. After pouring out everything in his heart, He asked me if I had anything to say for myself. I told him that I had a letter for him to read. Nervously, I handed him the letter. As his eyes moved back and forth surveying the words of my letter, for the first time in my life I saw God change the heart of a man. And He used my letter, of all things, to do it. The look on his face was priceless. He asked me to leave the room. I wanted to do cartwheels as I walked into that hallway. I praised God realizing at that moment what He had done for me. After a while, my boss called me back into his office. He said to me that he wasn't going to fire me. He told me that I could stay on as long as I didn't miss any more days and was on time. Of course, I agreed. He ended our meeting with the same harsh scolding at its beginning.

It was at the end of the workday after I finally left his office. Immediately, I went to my pastor's home to recap all that happened. Their advice to me was to dry my tears, take the whipping, and be grateful for God's mercy. They reminded me that God chastises those that He loves, so I dried my tears, praised God for His faithfulness, grace, and mercy, and I went on to finish my degree. I kept myself free of abusive relationships, but there was still a deep pain that I had to endure. I still didn't want to face being alone. I knew that God was calling for a kind of brokenness to occur in me which would change my perspective of being alone. But I was afraid and, quite frankly, had no desire to go through that pain and isolation. Acutely aware of the brokenness that I was about to endure, my hands extended toward heaven and my heart sank within me. "Father, not my will but thy will be done"; this was my second response. Initially, I screamed, "I've gone through enough pain; must I face this too? Must I face the isolation?" It was at this point that I desired to run. But as soon as my feet left the block, I was miserable. That day my prayer was, "Father, I choose not to go through this valley. Please don't box me in like you did, Jonah. Let me choose."

After this prayer, I began my marathon. My running was accompanied by tears, despair, and silence. I still went to church, but I didn't pray, I didn't read my word, and I was a pew warmer. I wanted to talk to my heavenly Father because I missed him, but I didn't want to hear Him reject what I wanted, so I went on running. My Pastor would call, church friends, and ministers, as well, but their calls went unanswered. It was at this time that the women from my church went looking for me.

The women that went on this search for me had no idea where I lived, except that I lived in a neighboring city. Nonetheless, they were bent on finding me. Unfortunately, they were unable to locate my whereabouts. Those few weeks felt like hell on earth. I can't find the words to describe the separation that I felt from my Father, my God, my Savior, and my guide. The pain was more than excruciating. I turned my attention to this pain that I found myself experiencing and thought, *what a way to avoid pain!* The very thing I tried to avoid, I sprinted toward with great speed. I reconciled within myself that pain with purpose is better than pain in vain. The pain would be experienced either way by trusting God or running. Pain resulting from obedience is far better than the pain of disobedience. The first brings life and life more abundantly, and the other brings death. It was at this moment that things became clear.

A simple choice needed to be made - choose life or choose death. In choosing life, I fell to my knees and asked the Father to forgive me. He so lovingly said, "Fear not; for I am with you be not dismayed; for I am your God: I will strengthen you; yes, I will help you; yes, I will uphold you with the right hand of my righteousness. I have blotted out, as a thick cloud, your transgressions, and, as a cloud, your sins: return unto me: for I have redeemed you" (Isaiah 41:10, 44:22, KJV).

Our Father wouldn't be a loving Father if He did not chastise His children. So, he goes on to say, "But you have not called on me...; but you hast been weary of me...I will work, and who shall let [hinder] it? I have formed thee; ...you will not be forgotten of me" (Isaiah 43:13, 21, 22, KJV). I was reminded that God would perfect those things that concerned me. I rose to my feet, and the next Sunday, my face was found at church. My pastors were concerned, as well as others. I received an admonishment from my pastors and the ministers to not forsake assembling myself with the congregation of faith and to stay in touch. I didn't go into detail about what I was experiencing, but I promised to stay in touch. Shortly thereafter, I moved to Tuskegee, where my church is located.

Since writing the letter that God used to shift the heart of my boss, I began to write more and more. I took a freelancing job with a magazine in a local city and was very excited to see my writing in print. It was happening. My childhood dream of being a writer was coming true. I later began writing the church newsletter. I was grateful for all that God had delivered me from, and even more grateful that He had given me the opportunity to encourage others, but they're still there remained very serious issues that I had not dealt with. Nevertheless, I continued living.

In 2009, my high school sweetheart and I reconnected. It was funny how it happened. One night I dreamt of him standing with a baseball cap on his head. He came up to me in the dream and hugged me. The next morning, I woke up with him on my mind. I decided to look up his sister in the neighboring city to find out how he was. Hoping I had the right number, I called and left a message for his sister to call me. Not long after, I received a callback. It was my high school sweetheart. He explained how excited he was to see my name on the caller ID. He wasn't sure that it was me calling, but he hoped it was. He further explained that he'd been divorced for over a year and how things were going in his life since the divorce. We decided to meet at a local pizza parlor to catch up. Through the window of the parlor, I could see him walk up the sidewalk to the entrance. He was still very handsome. Once inside, he greeted me with a hug. With the warmth of his embrace, I felt like I was that teenage girl again. I felt a familiar comfort come over me that I remembered as a teenager whenever he would embrace me. He later met my children and not long after, we began dating.

He accompanied me to church, attending prayer every week and worship service every Sunday. I was in heaven. Finally, a man I could rock with spiritually. Eventually, he joined the church and often talked with Pastor about how he could be of service. A great relationship developed between us, my children, and his children. Upon our children's meeting, they became each other's biggest fans. It was beautiful. Our courtship was beautiful. We spent time talking and praying together. He would often read the bible to me while I reclined against his chest. I felt such peace with him.

Within three months of our courtship, he came to me and said that he believed God wanted us to marry. He wanted to know if I received any indication from God that we should marry. I told him that I was experiencing an extraordinary peace with him that I had not experienced with any other man in my life. I believed the peace to be God-sent, but now in retrospect, it would have been wise to wait. Not because I was unsure, but because the wait to marry would have allowed time for both our financial and emotional situations to improve and it would have allowed us time to develop a strong foundation for our relationship. Not long after our discussion, he pro- posed during a Sunday morning church service. We were called to the front of the church, right below the altar. I had no idea why we were being summoned. Then he turned to me and told me how much he loved me and asked me to marry him. I was shaking! I never expected such an open proposal. I guess I always imagined a quiet evening over dinner, but this was very public. I nervously said yes, not because of the crowd, but because I loved him and felt that God was giving us a second chance.

We yielded ourselves to premarital counseling with my Pastor and his wife, and so commenced a new beginning different from anything that I have ever known, or at least I expected it to be different. In our counseling sessions, we discussed past issues of divorce, and abuse; anything and everything you could think of was placed on the table for discussion. We both walked away knowing that we had issues, but we also walked away willing to come together for better or worse. We married not long after. Shortly after our wedding, it seemed like all hell broke loose. His children were not allowed to visit with us since the day of the ceremony. After attempting on several occasions to have the children visit, my husband simply stopped trying because of the opposition from their mother. He was worn and frustrated.

Not seeing the children devastated him, and he slowly began to pull away. His job situation didn't help either. He was barely making enough money to cover his child support and other obligations. I could tell he felt inadequate as a man, but I tried to make things better by taking him out to cheer him up. But he continued to slowly pull away. The pain of rejection, loneliness, and depression quickly resurfaced in me. We often attended post-marital counseling with our pastors and afterward, for a few weeks at least, everything seemed better. Eventually, we would relive the previous weeks of estrangement. Childhood issues of rejection resurfaced for both of us. We both handled it as best we knew how. I compensated by trying to find comfort in him, which didn't work at all since he coped by withdrawing. Turning to food, I found solace as well as 20 extra pounds! The conflict was very much alive in our home, and it was suffocating. In tears, I threw up my hands, approached my husband of eight months, and asked him to leave. Deep down this wasn't what I desired. I longed to connect with him again, to communicate in a loving way and receive loving communication from him.

Sadly, we allowed so many things to get in the way of losing our way back to each other. We'd become strangers sharing the same house. It was the enemy's words that prevailed in my mind, telling me we would not succeed in this marriage.

Our separation ended in divorce in 2010. The decision to end our marriage was not God's best. I made a mess, expecting our heavenly Father to clean it up. Sometimes, by His grace and mercy, He lifts us out of the middle of our own making and guides us along a better path if we let him. At other times, He gives us the grace to go through the consequences of our messes. This was one of those messes that I would have to endure with God's grace. Divorcing my husband brought much sorrow to my heart. I prayed for forgiveness. While I worked through the pain of my divorce, the Lord spoke to me and said, "Strengthen those things which remain." It was a daily fight to turn my attention away from the loss of my spouse, but I did as the Lord said - I strengthened my children by being attentive to what they needed spiritually and physically. I resolved to follow the Lord and supported my local church by being available to assist in any way that I could. For seven years, I journeyed the path of self-improvement believing that my best life would begin with a better me.

Chapter 5
God Turns Rough Roads into Beautiful Destinations

> I had fainted unless I had believed to see the goodness of the LORD in the land of the living.
> Psalms 27:13 (kjv)

Years passed, but my desire to be a wife hadn't. The hope for a godly partner never died. It withered a few times, but the flame flickered on. Often, I prayed for a man whose heart could be touched by the Spirit of God but soon realized the generality of this request. By faith, I believe there were tons of guys out there with David's testimony of being a man after God's own heart. I needed to hone in – get more specific. The goal was to stay away from creating a list of superfluous traits like a chiseled body and a dashing smile. Not to say that there's anything wrong with that, but I had 'that guy' and still found myself wanting.

It was necessary for me to drill down into the kind of character I wanted my future husband to possess not forsaking a heart after God but adding the traits of a champion. My GOAT (Greatest of All Time) would be one who would promote the interest of God, and be courageous, loving, and supportive. He would embody integrity, discipline, and hard work. Of equal importance, I wanted to get my "Grown Woman" on - be a wise, strong, and fearless woman, a great wife, and a humble participant in building our life together.

My #grownWomangoals called for me to be courageous, bold in Christ, more loving, more patient, and gentler, but I struggled to manifest this person. Over time the responsibility of facing the issues of single parenting caused me to become rough around the edges. The hurt of past relationships caused me to be less courageous and bold. The everyday struggle of simply surviving hardened me causing a less gentle side to emerge. I'll admit, back then, I wasn't the easiest person to love, and to make matters worse, I was thirsty for love. The unresolved hurt in my life produced by one relationship after another compounded and left me dry, bitter, and full of emptiness. An awareness of my desperate need for wholeness and healing poured into my consciousness as hot metal poured into a mold; but like most of us, I simply ignored the call to be shaped into a vessel of strength that would sharpen and receive refinement from my community of believers and ultimately my mate. It's no wonder when the Lord in His creative and humbling way called me to his forge to craft and authenticate me into his divine nature. I desperately needed it.

Fix Your Dress

Oftentimes God uses movies to simplify a message he wants to convey to me. I love these moments when he causes the light bulb of my spirit to illuminate with practical wisdom and understanding. Ms. Oprah calls these instances of clarity "Aha" moments. One night while watching a scene from *Laws of Attraction*, a romantic comedy released in 2004, I received such enlightenment. In this movie, there are two high-profile divorce attorneys - one male and the other female - who each represent a distressed couple – a rock star husband, and a fashion designer wife. The scene starts with a high-profile female divorce attorney, Audrey Woods, walking out of an evening rock concert she attends with her groupie mother. She's obviously annoyed by the ear-splitting music and packed crowd. After finding space to breathe and shake off her annoyance, she hears the designer's wife cursing and crying. With a concerned tone, she approaches her and asks what's wrong. The fashion designer wife spouts off about her rockstar husband – the on-stage performer in the concert Audrey just left - being a serial cheater and how she can't trust him. The divorce attorney comforts her and offers her services. After gathering herself emotionally, the fashion designer's wife notices the divorce attorney is wearing a red dress from her collection. She informs the attorney that she's wearing it wrong. The attorney, oblivious to this fact, says, "Oh," and adjusts the dress to wear it as designed. End of scene.

The Lord whispered in my ear, one morning during prayer and said, "You're wearing my dress wrong." Perplexed, I responded, "What dress, Lord? I'm wearing pants." He continued; "you're wearing my dress wrong. It wasn't designed to fit the way you're wearing it." It finally occurred to me that he wasn't talking about the actual clothing I had on. So, I listened. The Lord continued; "I've dressed you...clothed you with womanhood. But you're wearing it wrong." If you're like me, needing a scriptural basis for such a word, turn to, Genesis 2:8, which reads, *And the Lord God said, It is not good that man should be alone; I will make him an help meet for him.* That word "make" gets my attention. So, I delve in and find its Hebrew counterpart. The Hebrew word for "make" is ʿāśâ, which lists one of its meanings as "to dress." The helpmeet was getting a dress! And what was that helpmeet called? You guessed it – WOMAN! If you still have any doubt that womanhood is a dress, look specifically, at Genesis 2:22, which reads, *"And the rib, which the Lord God has taken from man, made him a woman...* There's that word made again! The Father took a man's rib and dressed it, adorned it, and clothed it with a woman.

Understanding now that the dress God was referring to was not any cotton on my back but the very flesh of my body, I humbled myself and asked, Father, "How am I incorrectly wearing that which you have dressed me in?" Is that your prayer? Do you want our Father, to reveal to you how you're wearing what he has so creatively and beautifully adorned you with? Now, wait, when you ask just be prepared for things to get a little heavy or not. At this point, it got real for me.

Womanhood as a Commodity

Imagine going to a pawnshop and handing the store clerk one of your breasts or your leg only for him to haggle some demeaning price that lowers your head and sinks your heart. Surprisingly, you agree with his assessment not because you want to but because there's some desperate situation that demands this sacrifice be made. You make the trade - money for a treasure - and walk away. This is difficult to imagine but what if I told you that we as women do this daily? We pawn our legs, our mouths, our breasts, our vaginas, our trust, and our emotional health for a rent check, light bill money, or some promise of security, exclusivity, or even marriage. We treat our femininity as some common, ordinary thing instead of the extraordinary possession it is. We remove the "handle with care" markers of our souls and bodies and allow our womanhood to be treated as clay pots rather than refined gold. We do this when we betray ourselves by conforming to someone else's image of us instead of affixing our eyes upon God to behold our likeness and portray this image to the world. We become complicit when we stay in abusive relationships, sell ourselves for a quick buck, and give away our power by not speaking up for ourselves. You might say, well I don't do any of those things. Sis, please know that this is not an extensive list. I promise you; you will discover your complicity before the end of this book.

We have focused a lot on the verbal and physical abuse of a partner. Yet, it is necessary to discuss the verbal and physical abuse we heap upon ourselves as women. How can we possibly get our "grown woman" on when we beat ourselves down with negative self-talk? That locks down our spirit. It's how we love ourselves that will dictate to others how we're to be loved. We're not exempt from treating our womanhood as a commodity when we live fearful and distrustful lives. Will we fall short at times? Yes, but the freedom we have in God is that we can adjust our dress as many times as needed to wear it the way God intends. When we receive the revelation of our worth as women, those times of needing to adjust our dress become less and less. Wearing our womanhood is much like hitting that goal weight. We won't get there by fad dieting or just having a desire to fit in a certain dress size! It's deeper than that. We lose weight and keep it off by adjusting our mindsets and disciplining our bodies which leads to better health and well-being. We will see our dress needing fewer adjustments when we kick the fad diets like compromising ourselves just to avoid loneliness. Don't read these words and act like you don't know what I'm talking about. I'm referring to those fad diets like booty calls every now and again! I'm talking about those quick fixes like that sugar daddy you hit up when the rent is due! I'm talking about somebody else's husband that you DM because you've given up hope that God will ever give you your own husband. When we know our worth, we need no more adjustments.

Know Your Worth

To know something signifies that we are aware of, acquainted with, and understand it. To know our worth, it is imperative that we know our design and the <u>One</u> who designed us. Formed and made are two verbs used in scripture to describe God's work of creating a man and a woman. You see, unlike man who was formed in Genesis 2:7, we women were made (Gen. 2:22). Both words (formed and made) are somewhat similar but there's a twist. Both words imply something created. However, "form" which is *yatsar* in Hebrew, means "to squeeze into shape." On the other hand, bānâ, the Hebrew word for "make" means "to build." One is squeezed into shape and the other is built. It's the difference between building a house and shaping pottery. One process is not better than the other, it's just different. Therefore, what is created through these processes is not better or less than the other. We're simply different but created by the same God.

My job here is not to juxtapose men and women. This comparison is pointless being that I, a woman, would still have no greater knowledge of myself by measuring myself to a man or even another woman for that matter. Our worth is not found in comparison only in the awareness and appreciation of one's own design. We know we were all created in the image of God - male and female alike. However, when God created woman, he went about it in a slightly different way. We're composed like a beautiful symphony. Yet, even Beethoven's most famous piano concerto is no comparison to God's design of a woman.

Ultimately, the hand of God molds us into the woman he desires, but there are other influences at work. Our environments shape our perspectives of the world around us and even ourselves for better or for worst. The violence of my home environment in my formative years fashioned me into a frightened, man-pleasing, and docile little girl who perceived men to be this mix of love and hate. This perspective is what ultimately caused me to settle with abuse in my life.

As a young woman, the feelings of being abandoned by my biological father and abusive relationships molded me into a love-thirsty, rough around the edges survivalist who trusted no one and felt I had to defend myself against everyone. Oh, but let all the believers say, "But God!" As the old saints would say, "If it had not been for the Lord on my side, where would I be?" The answer to this question is easy. I'd be dead. I praise God that the experiences of my youth didn't have the final say and neither does yours. Ultimately, the hand of God reshapes us - remaking us into his masterpiece. Somebody say, "I got to be made!" Today is the day when we put away our childish ways of thinking and acting to know the worth of our design.

The Word of God sheds light on how we should wear our dress of womanhood. Womanhood is meant to be worn with strength, honor, dignity, wisdom, and kindness as seen in Proverbs 31. When I read about this Proverbs 31 woman in times past, I admit, I was a little intimidated. This woman has her ducks in a row and shooting 'em down!

She ain't playing with yawl. She's a wife, mother, and businesswoman who is always prepared, and always scaling up as seen with her profitable trading. She's industrious making clothes and giving to the poor. This woman has it going on. But before I understood what this woman was meant to do, she intimidated me.

This woman seems to be able to do it all without blunder. However, this estimation was not true. She couldn't do it all. She excelled in what was given to her to specifically do according to her gifts and abilities. She was gifted with a husband; therefore, she excelled as a wife. You may be gifted with singleness and excel in expressing this gift in your life. She was gifted with children and servants and excelled at running her home. You may be gifted with a cute puppy and a cozy apartment. Excel at caring for your home and your pets.

This Proverb 31 woman was a realtor with a good eye for the property being able to "consider a field and buy it...." You may be gifted as an artist or an engineer, a musician, or a writer. Excel in that gift. You get the point, right? It's not about living up to the image and ability of this woman but it's about allowing this woman to inspire you to utilize your gifts and callings to live up to who you were meant to be.

Our worth is derived from and set in God who is unchangeable. This means my worth should never change. Our worth is not designed to go up and down like the stock market. Our worth is not designed to fluctuate shining brightly one moment and dimly the next. Whether with children or not, our worth stays the same. Whether rich or poor, my worth stays the same. Whether married or single, our worth stays the same. Whether success or failure, our worth doesn't shift. Whether a man loves us or hates us, our worth doesn't change. Our worth lies in God who has said before the foundations of the world that I am fearfully and wonderfully made. God himself paid the ransom for our lives and said that our lives are worthy enough of His life. God has made us so worthy that he sings over us every day. He crowns us daily with love and compassion. And even when we die, we still have worth as the Father receives us unto himself. This is the jewel of worth that God has placed upon and within us.

Our worth doesn't change because we don't see it. Oh my God, I thank Daddy God for seeing my worth even when I didn't. I thank him that he didn't leave me blind to my own worth but that he showed me that I was worthy enough to sleep next to my husband and not a man that I thought I needed. I thank God that he found me worthy of enough being made in His image. Even in my error, God finds me worthy enough to receive correction. Even in sin, God finds me worthy enough to extend His forgiveness and die on that roughed cross. And because of the worth God alone has placed upon my life, Father God is more than worthy of my life's praise and worship. Amen!

The Lord is saying to you, "you are the apple of my eye – precious, comparable only to fine gold. Let nothing and no one separate you from knowing your worth that you've been reminded of today." Now begins the difficult work of inner healing where God promises to turn our rough roads into beautiful destinations. Inner healing looks different for many people. For me, it means freedom from past mistakes, wholeness of spirit, mind, and body which brings an end to double-mindedness, and freedom from the betrayal of the person I desire to be. This is not the end, but the beginning of transformative change for me as I hope it will be for you. Let's shift our thinking together and dare to believe that with God, we can make it out and break the cycle of abuse!

I pray that this book has inspired you to know that God is no respecter of persons. If He did it for me by turning my life and the lives of my children around, he will surely do it for you!

Peace & blessings!

www.ingramcontent.com/pod-product-compliance
Lightning Source LLC
LaVergne TN
LVHW040158080526
838202LV00042B/3219